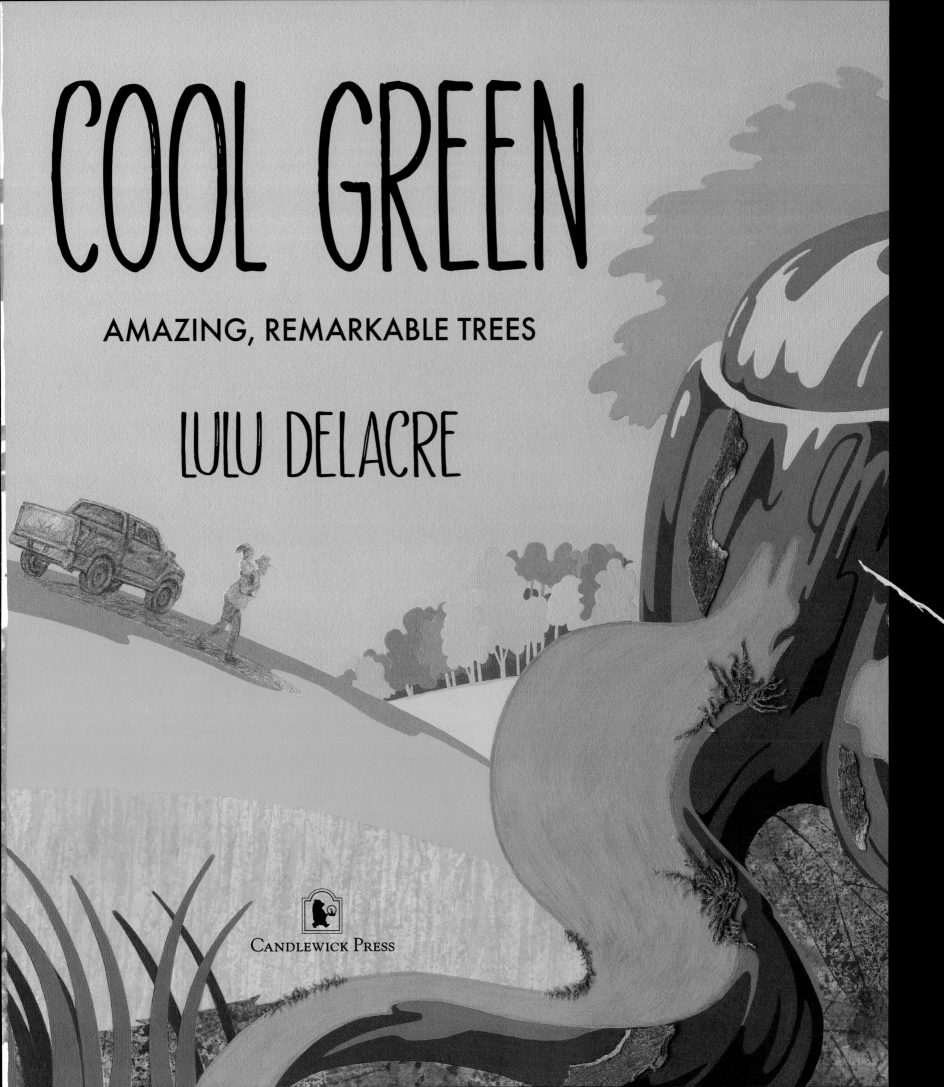

COOL GREEN

AMAZING, REMARKABLE TREES

LULU DELACRE

CANDLEWICK PRESS

¿Por qué, abuelo? Why?

Why am I in awe of trees?
Trees are astounding!
Let me share with you, mi niña,
some of the reasons why.

Hidden, huddled,
among others of its kind,
only a handful of humans
have ever glimpsed it:
a coast redwood towers
above every single one
of the three trillion living trees
on planet Earth.

In an ancient
forest of red giants,
General Sherman reigns supreme.
More than two thousand years old,
it is the world's biggest
clean air machine.

A symphony
of birds and bees
make their home
in the thickest of all trees,
an ahuehuete.
In its rugged bark,
el árbol del Tule hides
imaginary creatures
for you to seek.

By day, it soaks in the sun.
By night, it bathes in sea breeze.
Tree of life,
tree of plenty,
tree of one thousand uses:
the coconut tree.
A palm with a drupe,
a coconut—
a sweet fruit, hard nut,
and the world's
second-largest seed!

The monkey puzzle
is a living fossil
and cousin of trees
from long ago.
Its scale-like leaves
on snake-like branches
can live to be
twenty-four years old!

Ah, I love the baobab,
an upside-down tree
with a trunk like a sponge.
In a downpour, its belly swells.
In a drought, its belly shrinks.

Then, just in the summer
and just for one night,
its white hanging bells,
laden with sweet-sour scent,
lure bats from beyond.

Have you heard of the amazing umbrella thorn acacia?

Not only does it dress its branches
with needles and hooks;
it also pumps poison
straight to its leaves
to ward off the grazers
in search of fresh lunch.
This neighborly neighbor
sends signals of scent
to warn nearby acacias
of foragers feeding away.

As the bark peels,
new colors appear,
ice blue and purple,
hot orange and red,
bitter yellow and green.
The rainbow gum gleams!
Mother Nature's
ever-changing masterpiece
never repeats.

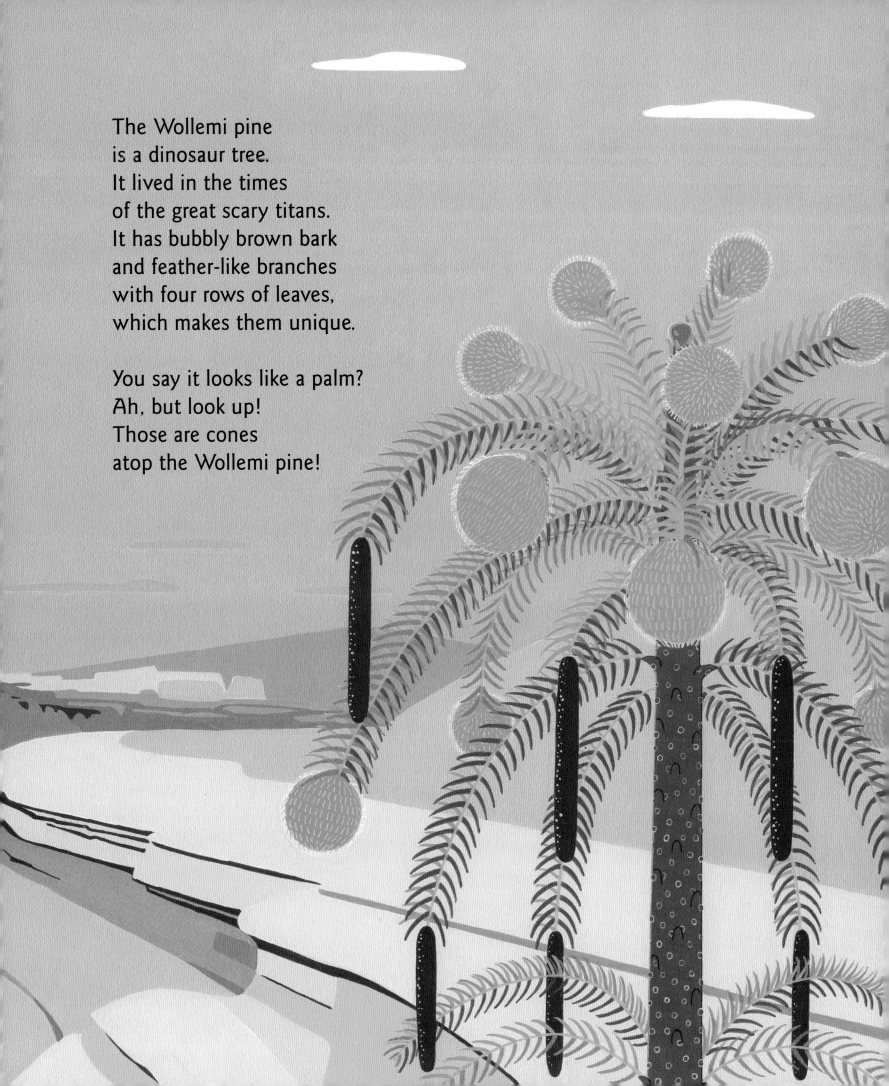

The Wollemi pine
is a dinosaur tree.
It lived in the times
of the great scary titans.
It has bubbly brown bark
and feather-like branches
with four rows of leaves,
which makes them unique.

You say it looks like a palm?
Ah, but look up!
Those are cones
atop the Wollemi pine!

Mother trees rule in the woods.
They care for their young,
shielding them from the sun
so seedlings grow slow and strong.
They are old and wise,
opening their roots
and welcoming inside
just the right fungi.

And mushrooms and trees
give and receive
nutrients and notes,
talking in chemical code.
This intricate network
of fungal filaments
is the wondrous wood-wide web!

The mighty moringa
is a miracle tree.
So many nutrients
in its fern-like big leaves.
Toss them into a salad
for a peppery bright lunch.
Steam its green pods
like asparagus.
Roast its peanut-like seeds.
A tree quite easy to grow.
It will thrive in poor soil
and do well in dry spells.
It loves dry and hot sun
all year long!

Abuelo,
Moringuita is my favorite tree!

Trees are cool green, mi niña.
As long as we care for them,
they'll care for us.

A NOTE FROM THE AUTHOR-ILLUSTRATOR

There are many more remarkable trees beyond the ones that appear in this book. I could have included the tallest tropical flowering tree, a yellow meranti named Menara, in Malaysian Borneo, a tree I learned about during my research. However, I came to the conclusion that by limiting the selection, I was opening the door to young readers to ask themselves which trees are most remarkable to them and why.

My favorite tree is *Moringa oleifera*. It's a visually humble tree with powerful healing and nourishing properties. As part of my research for this book, I grew my own Moringuita from seed. And after learning of the symbiotic relationship between trees and fungi, I inoculated oak logs with shiitake spawn and grew my own fresh shiitake mushrooms.

Research also led me to learn about identifying trees by the kinds of leaves they produce. This is why I sought real leaves from the trees mentioned in the book to embed into the art. It is my way of bringing the specific trees closer to the reader, hoping to prompt them to collect, press, and identify tree leaves, just as I did.

Is your favorite tree in this book? Or is yours one that is not included? If you don't live near the native range of some of the trees mentioned in the book, look for them at your nearest arboretum or botanical garden. You might be surprised by what you find! And I encourage you to plant your own tree seed. Each seed has a potential amazing remarkable tree in it, if you only nurture it.

WHY TREES?

More than seventy-three thousand species of trees inhabit the Earth. Of this number, some nine thousand species are believed to be rare, undiscovered, and likely living in remote tropical lowlands and mountains. Trees are the lungs of the planet. They protect the land from erosion. They encourage rainfall. They provide food and shelter. They are witnesses of history. They are beautiful. They make the Earth a cool place to live.

Trees purify the air we breathe. Forests (large groups of trees) reduce damaging greenhouse gases when they turn carbon dioxide into oxygen. Trees harness the energy of the sun and use it to combine carbon and hydrogen into sugars. They take carbon from the carbon dioxide gas in the air. They take hydrogen from the water they drink. In the process of combining both to produce sugars, they release the oxygen they can't use into the air. The oxygen that trees release supports people and other animals. Any extra sugars the trees do not consume right away end up stored in their trunks!

Tree trunks record climate changes. The rings of an ancient tree trunk tell the age of the tree as well as what the climate was like during a specific time. There is a ring for each year, and the rings' widths vary according to how warm, wet, cold, or dry it was during that time.

Trees' root systems protect people from river floods. Their thick roots branch out into flexible tendrils that help hold the soil around the trees in place. This system acts as a net that regulates the flow of groundwater. By holding the soil in place, the roots keep the soil from washing into a river, where it would displace the water; this helps reduce the risk of the river bursting its banks.

Trees' leaves catch rain and let it evaporate into clouds. Evaporation cools down the atmosphere. Clouds bring rain to someplace where it is needed. Trees' fallen leaves become a great soil conditioner. When a tree's leaves change color and fall to the ground, the tree is said to be deciduous, while an evergreen tree stays green all the time. Trees provide shade, food, and shelter for wildlife and people. Many mammals, birds, insects, reptiles, and even fish depend on trees for survival.

Trees are enduring, respectful, and beautiful. Long-lived trees are witnesses to historical events worth remembering. Trees are an example of peaceful coexistence in the forest. Scientists have proven that trees communicate with one another, helping one another survive, sometimes even keeping a stump alive! Trees are beautiful living things to look at and are a source of inspiration. Reading under a tree, drawing a tree, or observing a tree brings calm and fosters serenity.

COOL FACTS ABOUT THE TREES IN THIS BOOK

LIVING STUMPS

Sometimes you find a living tree stump in the forest. How can a tree live without leaves to produce food or a trunk to store nutrients? A neighboring tree of the same species may have grafted, or joined, its roots to the felled tree. This keeps the stump alive for many years as sugars and nutrients from the linked tree flow into it. Scientists believe that this link between trees may benefit the neighboring tree as well, since the grafts allow the neighbor to expand its root network and get access to water and nutrients from a larger soil area.

WHITE OAK WITNESS TREE

Quercus alba, deciduous
In 2004, the oak was selected as America's national tree. More than sixty species of oaks grow in the United States. Hailed for their beauty, lumber, and shade, oaks are also long-lived.

Many have been witnesses to important events in American history. Near Stone Bridge, in Manassas National Battlefield Park, in Virginia, stands a white oak that witnessed the Civil War battles there in 1861 and 1862.

COAST REDWOOD

Sequoia sempervirens, evergreen
Coast redwoods are towering, long-lived trees native to the Pacific Northwest. They grow slowly and, resistant to both fire and decay, can live up to two thousand years. The tallest living tree is a coast redwood reaching 380 feet (115.6 meters). Seventy percent of known trees over 350 feet (107 meters) tall worldwide are coast redwoods growing at Humboldt Redwoods State Park, in California. Steve Sillett, a botanist and forester who has climbed champion trees, says that the only protection for these rare individuals, who cannot run and hide, is anonymity.

GENERAL SHERMAN

Giant sequoia (*Sequoiadendron giganteum*), evergreen
This giant sequoia boasts some impressive numbers. Located in the Sequoia National Park, in Tulare County, California, it's the biggest living tree in the world based on its estimated total wood volume. Fifty-five percent of a giant sequoia's mass is in its trunk, and General Sherman weighs about 1,385 tons (1,256 metric tons)! General Sherman is believed to be about 2,200 years old and is a survivor of the massive 2021 wildfires.

EL ÁRBOL DEL TULE

Ahuehuete (*Taxodium mucronatum*), evergreen
Ahuehuete means "old man of the water" in the Indigenous language Nahuatl. Also called the Montezuma bald cypress, this tree thrives in swamplands and along streambanks. It is native to Mexico and Guatemala.

El árbol del Tule is an ahuehuete tree located in the small town of Santa María de Tule in Oaxaca, Mexico. Legend says that Ehecatl, the Aztec god of wind, planted it for the local inhabitants, and some of the locals consider it sacred. It measures almost 120 feet (more than 36 meters) around its trunk, and it takes seventeen people with outstretched arms to surround it! Many more people can take shelter under its crown, which is 144 feet (44 meters) wide.

COCONUT PALM

Cocos nucifera, evergreen
Native to Southeast Asia and the islands between the Indian and Pacific Ocean, coconut palms are propagated by seed. The large seed is dispersed by gravity, seawater, and people. It is believed that Europeans brought coconuts to the Americas. The coconut palm now thrives in eighty countries, including the islands in the Caribbean.

The coconut is a drupe, a one-seeded fruit with three main layers: the skin, the flesh, and the stony pit. In the coconut's case, the outer skin is green, the middle layer is fibrous instead of fleshy, and the inner layer is a hard shell that contains the large seed. The seed, initially hollow, produces coconut water and flesh as it grows.

Every layer of the coconut is used for something somewhere in the world. Rope, doormats, brushes, and mattress stuffing are made from the husk's fibers. Husk fibers are also burned to ward off mosquitoes and ground to make cosmetics. People make masks, containers, musical instruments, and ornaments out of the dried shell. The coconut seed's flesh is shaved for desserts, ground for flour, and squeezed for milk and oil. And coconut water, from green immature coconuts, is a delicious thirst quencher!

MONKEY PUZZLE TREE

Araucaria araucana, evergreen
The monkey puzzle tree, also called the piñonero or pehuén, is Chile's national tree. The English common name comes from a comment made by a guest at a dinner party in Victorian England. While being shown the rare tree by its well-to-do owner, the guest commented that it would "puzzle a monkey" to climb the tree's spiky branches. (An impossible puzzle, since there are no monkeys in the areas where the trees occur naturally!)

Monkey puzzle trees are linked to similar species of trees found in prehistoric fossils from the time when South America, Antarctica, and Australia were one continent. When young, the tree has a pyramidal shape. However, as it ages, it loses its bottom branches, giving it a top-heavy appearance. Scientists believe that its thick bark is an adaptation that protects the tree from volcanic lava flow. Its leaves are leathery and spiky. Its cones' seeds are like large pine nuts and are a staple of the Pehuenche people, for whom the tree is sacred. The monkey puzzle lives up to one thousand years and is related to the Wollemi pine.

BAOBAB

Adansonia digitata, deciduous
The baobab tree is native to Africa. It is sometimes called the upside-down tree, because when it loses all its leaves in winter, it looks upside down, with bare branches that look like roots. Its tender, pale wood shows no growth rings, so it's hard to know how old any one tree is. As they age, baobabs become hollow. Then people use them for water storage and shelter. Some baobabs can store up to 26,000 gallons (98,000 liters) of water in their barrel-like trunk!

Baobabs bloom in summer. Their heavy flowers can reach 5 inches (12.5 centimeters) across. The flowers bloom for only one night between dusk and dawn. They emit a sweet scent that changes to the smell of decaying flesh as the flowers wither. It's this foul smell that attracts fruit bats, which pollinate the flowers.

UMBRELLA THORN ACACIA

Acacia tortilis, evergreen
The umbrella thorn acacia is native to Africa and Arabia and thrives in the African savanna. Locals in Kenya make porridge with its pods and eat its immature seeds. Its leaves are used as food for cattle and loved by grazing wild animals such as giraffes.

The umbrella thorn acacia is protected from grazers by sharp, straight thorns that can be 4 inches (10 centimeters) long, as well as by smaller claw-like ones. As a second line of defense, the trees send a poisonous substance called tannin to their leaves. At the same time, they warn neighboring acacias by releasing a gas into the air that can spread downwind up to 164 feet (50 meters) away! Neighboring acacias can then pump their own leaves with tannin to ward off any hungry grazers coming their way.

RAINBOW GUM

Eucalyptus deglupta, evergreen

The rainbow gum tree, also called the Mindanao gum, is native to Indonesia, Papua New Guinea, and the Philippines, making it the only eucalyptus tree native to the Northern Hemisphere. It can grow up to 250 feet (76 meters) tall. The tree has smooth orange-tinted bark that peels away in strips, revealing fresh neon-green bark underneath. As the newly exposed bark ages, it changes from green to blue, from blue to purple, from purple to pink, and from pink to orange or rust. This peeling and color changing occur in a gradual ongoing process; a tree never shows the same pattern twice.

WOLLEMI PINE

Wollemia nobilis, evergreen

The Wollemi pine was thought to be extinct until 1994, when Australian park officer David Noble noticed the unusual tree growing in a gorge of the Blue Mountains, in Australia. He picked up a branch for identification. The tree's palm-frond-like leaves were found to be identical to fossils dating to the late Jurassic, 150 million years ago.

The leaves are covered by a thin film that protects them from water loss. As temperatures drop, the pines go dormant and any growing buds develop waxy protective coatings called ice caps. This feature surely helped the tree survive many ice ages. The Wollemi pine develops new stems from its roots, allowing it to survive after drought, fire, or rockfall. This trait is probably the reason that there are two hundred identical siblings in the Blue Mountains grove where Noble found them! Wollemi pines have both round female cones and long male ones. Their bark resembles delicious bubbling hot chocolate.

MOTHER TREES

Mother trees are the biggest and oldest trees in a forest. They are linked to hundreds of surrounding trees through a network of fungal filaments below the ground. Due to their size and age, they have extensive root systems in relationship with a vast fungal network, which carries both information and resources. For example, when a mother tree dies, it sends defense signals and sugars to the seedlings and young trees connected to it. The warning signals help the seedlings and young trees adapt to changes in the environment that the mother tree has detected. It does this to increase the seedlings' and young trees' resilience and chances for survival.

THE WOOD-WIDE WEB

All living trees are in a symbiotic (close and mutually beneficial) relationship with belowground fungi. Specific types of fungi form relationships with specific species of trees through a network of fungal filaments. In Acadia National Forest, in Maine, for instance, the fly agaric fungus (recognizable by its red cap) is symbiotic with pine, spruce, fir, birch, cedar, and hemlock trees.

Fungi absorb their food from the soil. Trees take in sunlight and produce their food in the form of sugars through the process of photosynthesis. Trees also need nutrients such as phosphorous and nitrogen, which they have difficulty absorbing. Through the fungal network, fungi easily collect phosphorus and nitrogen from the soil and pass them along to trees. In exchange, the fungi absorb some of the trees' sugars, which they use for energy. The network of fungal filaments also increases trees' access to water.

MORINGA TREE

Moringa oleifera, deciduous

The moringa tree, native to India, is widely cultivated across tropical and subtropical regions of Africa, Asia, Latin America, Australia, and the United States. It's so widespread and popular that it boasts at least 160 common names. A drought-resistant and fast-growing small tree, it grows up to 26 feet (8 meters) in its first year and to an average height of 50 feet (15 meters) in the dry tropics.

Moringa is a nutrient-dense plant with abundant healing properties. Its leaves have a protein content about the same as powdered milk but are available at a fraction of the cost. In addition, the leaves contain compounds known as mustard oils, which are some of the most potent antioxidants known and can potentially be used to reduce inflammation, help with diabetes, lower high blood pressure, and prevent cancer. Crushed moringa seeds help eliminate 90 to 99 percent of bacteria in untreated water, and high-quality oil extracted from them is used to lubricate the fine machinery of watches and orbiting satellites. Since moringa trees grow in many poor countries with high malnutrition, organizations worldwide are using them to support nutritional intake.

FOR FURTHER EXPLORATION

American Conifer Society: https://conifersociety.org

American Forests: https://www.americanforests.org

Arbor Day Foundation: https://www.arborday.org

Monumental Trees: https://www.monumentaltrees.com

Plant for the Planet: https://www.plant-for-the-planet.org/en/home

Plants for a Future: https://pfaf.org

"The Secret Language of Trees," directed by Avi Ofer, Ted-Ed, July 2019, https://www.ted.com/talks/camille
_defrenne_and_suzanne_simard_the_secret_language_of_trees?language=en.

BIBLIOGRAPHY

Anderson, Kirk. "No Place to Run, No Place to Hide: Acacia Defense." GardenSMART. March 6, 2009. https://
www.gardensmart.tv/?p=articles&title=Acacia_Defense_Living_Desert.

Black, Stef. "The Incredible Acacia Tree Phenomenon." Southern Destinations. September 25, 2014. https://
www.southerndestinations.com/incredible-acacia-tree-phenomenon/.

Choi, Charles Q. "Tree Stump Stays Alive with a Little Help from Neighboring Trees." Inside Science. July 25,
2019. https://www.insidescience.org/news/tree-stump-stays-alive-little-help-neighboring-trees.

Debreczy, Zsolt, and István Rácz. "El Arbol del Tule: The Ancient Giant of Oaxaca." *Arnoldia*, Winter 1997
–1998. http://arnoldia.arboretum.harvard.edu/pdf/articles/475.pdf.

Dordel, Julia, dir. *Intelligent Trees*. Pattensen, Germany: Dorcon Film, 2016.

Evans, Kate. "Make It Rain: Planting Forests Could Help Drought-Stricken Regions." Forest News. July 23, 2012.
https://forestsnews.cifor.org/10316/make-it-rain-planting-forests-to-help-drought-stricken-regions?fnl=.

Gatti, Roberto Cazzolla, et al. "The Number of Tree Species on Earth." *Proceedings of the National Academy of
Sciences* 119, no. 6 (February 8, 2022). https://www.pnas.org/content/119/6/e2115329119.

"General Sherman, the Biggest Tree in the World." Monumental Trees. https://www.monumental-trees.com
/en/trees/giantsequoia/biggest_tree_in_the_world/.

"General Sherman Tree." National Park Service. https://www.nps.gov/places/000/general-sherman-tree.htm.

Gilman, Edward F., et al. "*Quercus alba*: White Oak." University of Florida, IFAS Extension. April 24, 2019.
https://edis.ifas.ufl.edu/publication/st541.

Gowda, Juan. "Spines of *Acacia tortilis*: What Do They Defend and How?" Oikos 77 (November 1996):
279–284. https://www.researchgate.net/publication/236152925_Spines_of_Acacia_tortilis_What_Do
_They_Defend_and_HowPMC5872761/.

Han, Andrew P. "Rainbow in a Tree." Science Friday. November 6, 2013. https://www.sciencefriday.com
/articles/rainbow-in-a-tree/.

Hughes, Sylvia. "Antelope Activate the Acacia's Alarm System." New Scientist. September 28, 1990. https://
www.newscientist.com/article/mg12717361-200-antelope-activate-the-acacias-alarm-system/.

Kou, Xianjuan, et al. "Nutraceutical or Pharmacological Potential of *Moringa oleifera* Lam." *Nutrients* 10, no. 3
(March 12, 2018): 343. https://pubmed.ncbi.nlm.nih.gov/29534518/.

Olson, Mark E. "*La ciencia detrás de Moringa, el árbol milagro*." Seminar, Instituto de Biología de la

Universidad Nacional Autónoma de México. Streamed live on August 4, 2020, Seminarios IB, YouTube. https://www.youtube.com/watch?v=vdPOYHHNttU.

Olson, M. E. "Moringa: Frequently Asked Questions." *Acta Horticulturae* 1158 (2018), 19–32. https://doi.org/10.17660/ActaHortic.2017.1158.4.

Olson, M. E., and J. W. Fahey. "*Moringa oleifera*: Un árbol multiusos para las zonas tropicales secas." *Revista Mexicana de Biodiversidad* 82, no. 4 (2011), 1071–1082.

Pakenham, Thomas. *Le tour du monde en 80 arbres*. Paris: Hachette, 2019. (First published as *Remarkable Trees of the World*. New York: Norton, 2002.)

Pham, Laura J. "Coconut (*Cocos nucifera*)." *Industrial Oil Crops*, 2022. Science Direct. https://www.sciencedirect.com/topics/agricultural-and-biological-sciences/cocos-nucifera.

Price, Martin L. "The Moringa Tree." ECHO Technical Notes. Revised 2007. https://www.strongharvest.org/wp-content/uploads/2017/07/ECHO-Technical-Notes-The-Moringa-Tree-Dr.-Martin-Price.pdf.

Sillett, S. C., et al. "Increasing Wood Production Through Old Age in Tall Trees." *Forest Ecology and Management* 259 (2010), 976–994.

Simard, Suzanne. *Finding the Mother Tree: Discovering the Wisdom of the Forest*. New York: Knopf, 2021.

Snelling, Andrew A. "*Wollemia nobilis*: A Living Fossil and Evolutionary Enigma." Institute for Creation Research. April 1, 2006. https://www.icr.org/article/wollemia-nobilis-living-fossil-evolutionary-enigma.

Toomey, Diane. "Exploring How and Why Trees 'Talk' to Each Other." *Yale Environment 360*, September 1, 2016. https://e360.yale.edu/features/exploring_how_and_why_trees_talk_to_each_other.

"Traditional Crops: Moringa." Food and Agriculture Organization of the United Nations. https://www.fao.org/traditional-crops/moringa/en/.

"Trees"/"Nous Les Arbres." Fondation Cartier pour l'art contemporain, Paris. July 12, 2019 to January 5, 2020. https://www.fondationcartier.com/en/exhibitions/nous-les-arbres.

Wohlleben, Peter. *The Hidden Life of Trees*. Illustrated ed. Translated by Jane Billinghurt. Vancouver, BC, Canada: Greystone, 2018.

Yessis, Mike. "These Five 'Witness Trees' Were Present at Key Moments in America's History." *Smithsonian*, August 25, 2017. https://www.smithsonianmag.com/travel/these-five-witness-trees-were-present-at-key-moments-in-americas-history-180963925/.